黑克多去
马戏团

杰拉尔丁·麦克莱恩 著
N·多诺万 绘画

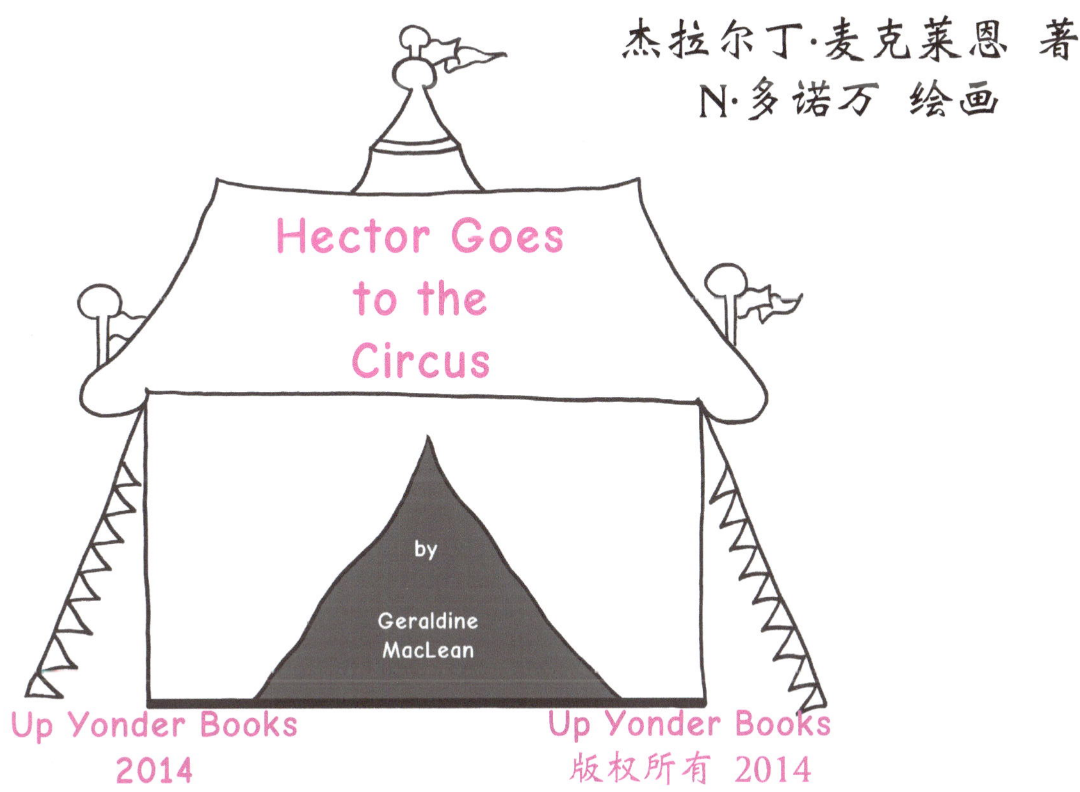

Up Yonder Books
www.upyonder.com
www.kids-lit.com

ISBN-13: 9780989484237
ISBN-10: 0989484238

献给布雷顿角的博伊斯戴尔的恩格思，
她非常喜欢她的小猪。

For Agnes of Boisdale, Cape Breton, who loved her pig.

Hector was the cheeriest piglet in the farmyard.

Mrs. Connors thought so and she was an expert on raising pigs and chickens and all sorts of farm critters.

黑克多是在农家院里最快乐的猪。

康纳斯夫人是这么想的，她是养猪、鸡和各种禽畜的专家。

N
E
W
S

Hector was the first pig
Mrs. Connors really loved
and whenever she came
to the barn, she tickled his
ears.

黑克多是康纳斯夫人第一个真正喜欢的
猪。每当她来到谷仓
黑克多给康纳斯夫人一个大大的
愉快的笑，而她挠他耳朵。

She scratched his belly
with his favourite stick.

她用他最喜欢的棍子撩他的肚子。

And she tweaked
his curly tail.

她还拧他卷卷的尾巴。

One September afternoon,
when Mr. and Mrs. Connors
were having tea and cupcakes,
Mr. Connors mentioned it
was time to sell Hector at
the Fall Fair.

九月的一个下午，
当康纳斯夫妇在喝茶和吃蛋糕，
康纳斯先生提到是时候在秋季集市时把黑克多掉了。

N
E
W

Mrs. Connors turned very quiet. She'd known all summer this day would come but dared not think about it. What could she do? She could not, would not, sell her beloved Hector to the highest bidder.

康纳斯夫人非常安静地转过身。整个夏天她已经知道这一天会到来，但从来不敢想。她能做什么？她不能、不想把她心爱的黑克多卖给出价最高的人。

康纳斯夫人有了一个绝妙的主意。

Mrs. Conners had a sparkling idea.

马戏团在镇上。也许，只是也许，黑克多可以加入它。
“你怎么认为呢，康纳斯先生？”

The circus was in town. Maybe, just maybe, Hector could join it.
"What do you think, Mr. Connors?"

Mr. Connors rubbed his chin and he scratched his head. He pulled on his right ear and Mrs. Connors knew he was thinking very hard.

"That is a very fine idea."

康纳斯先生摩擦着下巴，他挠了挠头，
他拉了拉他的右耳，
康纳斯夫人知道他在仔细地想。

"康纳斯夫人，你这个主意很好"。

The next day, Mrs. Connors explained everything to Hector as she washed his nose and scrubbed his feet. She brushed his coat till it shone and tied a green ribbon on his tail.

第二天，
康纳斯夫人洗他的鼻子和擦洗他的脚时，
向黑克多解释了一切。她刷洗他的毛皮，
直到它闪闪发光，
然后把一条绿色的丝带绑在他尾巴上。

When Hector was circus-ready,
Mr. and Mrs. Connors took
him to meet Mr. Banes, the ringmaster.

黑克多准备好去马戏团的时候，
康纳斯先生和夫人带他去见贝恩先生，
那里的驯兽师。

Mr. Banes noted Hector's wide smile and his perfect, tip-toe balance. "We have a winner!"

贝恩先生留意到黑克多笑容可掬以及他那完美的脚尖平衡技巧，

"我们有一个会成功的家伙!"

Every September after,
when the circus came to town,
Mr. and Mrs. Connors cheered
for Hector, the happiest pig in the world.

之后每年的9月份，
当马戏团来到小镇，
康纳斯夫妇为黑克多欢呼，
世界上最快乐的猪。

结束

THE END

其他故事:

Elswith the Witch。

交互式的动画图画书，在苹果App store。

Malky Joe in the Great Cruise Caper

在亚马逊网站上面有。

好玩，免费的法语课程，在苹果App store。搜索:

Learn French by Lessonstudio。

For more funny bone tickles,
search the Apple app store for interactive
and animated:

ELSWITH THE WITCH.

Check out Amazon Books for:

MALKY JOE IN THE GREAT CRUISE CAPER.

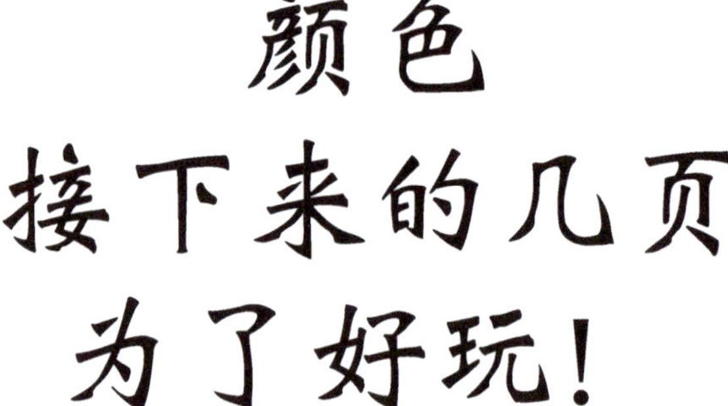

颜色
接下来的几页
为了好玩!

STEP RIGHT UP
AND COLOUR
THE NEXT PAGES
FOR FUN!!!

N
E
W
S

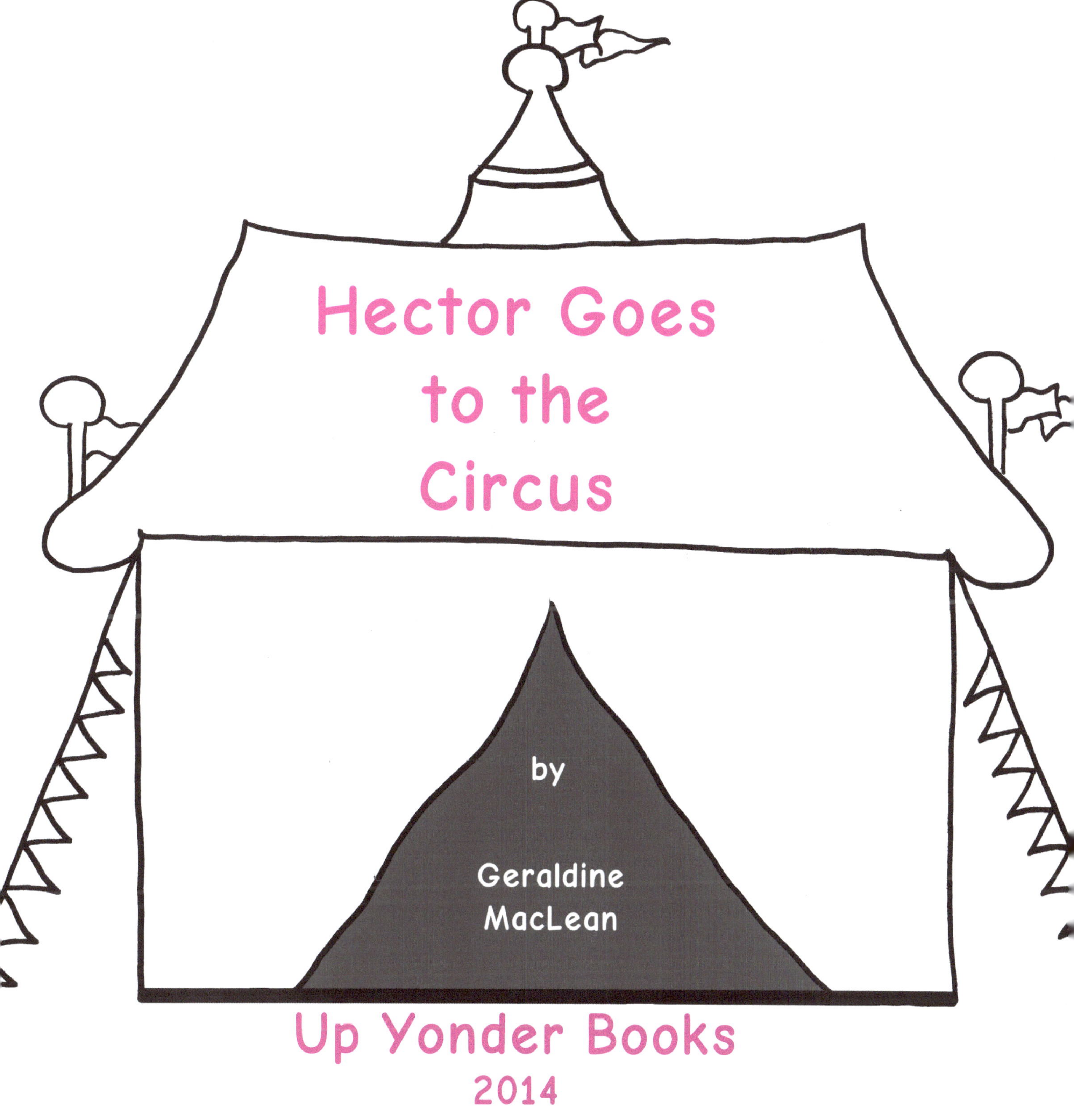
Hector Goes
to the
Circus
by
Geraldine
MacLean
Up Yonder Books
2014

www.ingramcontent.com/pod-product-compliance
Lightning Source LLC
LaVergne TN
LVHW070152230826
846093LV00002B/13

* 9 7 8 0 9 8 9 4 8 4 2 3 7 *